PRAYERS OF HONORING

VOICE

Written by Pixie Lighthorse

Lighthorse Publishing, 2017
Redmond, OR

Library of Congress Control Number: 2016920044

ISBN: 978-0-9982953-0-5

Cover design: Stacy de la Rosa
Layout: Twozdai Hulse

Lighthorse Publishing
SouLodge Ranch, LLC
Redmond, OR 97756
www.pixielighthorse.com

*For soul warriors who tend to their faith so
they are held as they tend the needs
of people and planet.*

CONTENTS

INTRODUCTION

Prayer has a way of clarifying what one is in service to. This book aims to strengthen the individual's voice through dialogue with the divine in order to reclaim it and put it to fair use. Having been robbed, repressed, manipulated, adjusted, shut down, and silenced for thousands of years, what comes out of the mouth isn't always clear or true. It is understandable, and it is also our responsibility to improve our communications with practice. Today there is a growing need for speaking clearly and with heart.

There is a mistaken notion that voice empowerment means one should speak every thought and complaint that blips across the mind, publicly and intimately. This book is not one of personal empowerment, rather it supports relational empowerment: the healing that comes from saying what heals and helps, thoughtfully and directed toward the source most likely to be able to witness the contents of the heart. Relational empowerment in this application focuses on building. Personal empowerment may or may not build; it can be destructive, mean, retaliating, mired in a loop of right and wrong, withholding, punishing, victimizing, and even abusive. Prayer has the potential to open up channels with the "Divine Source of Life as You Understand It" to begin a dialogue, which will hopefully lead to many fulfilling dialogues in your relationships.

I've found over and again that the reason for loss of voice is fear: of what someone will think of what we will think or believe about ourselves, what will happen to us if we speak up, and what floodgates might burst open if we turn the lid counter-clockwise on what we are feeling or have been through. There seems to be tremendous fear of telling our stories and being willing to vulnerably take ownership of them.

There are many things that are now ready to be said. It is time to heal what has been asking for medicine.

Rehabilitation of the voice can begin by taking a thorough

inventory of what is resting on the heart. Determining whether the matter found there is heavy, light, or neutral provides a moment of pause for considering what is liable to happen when an attempt is made to interpret it for the understanding of others. Fear usually speaks right up, and loudly. Silent resentment takes the place of naming expectations. Defensiveness abounds. Caustic inner dialogue makes turmoil of the gut. The body eventually tells the story of what has been relegated to the basement of the psyche with an assortment of symptoms and ailments.

Much courage is required to move beyond the usual narrative and into balance.

The throat, located just one energy center north of the heart and one jump south of the mind, is in a precarious position in the body. Play with me for a moment: if you were to consider the mind a machine, say, a telegraph in service to the heart, then the heart gives the first dictation. The mind then translates vital information in the form of language to the speaker system of voice, which will hopefully transmit the communications as the heart intended, if that is the priority. It is a good time to ask yourself what your priorities of communication are. What is motivating you?

A short journey from heart to mind and back down to the throat takes mere seconds, but a mighty many detours are taken en route. This may be because the fear residing in the mind is like a highwayman, waylaying our genuine matters of the heart and causing havoc as it tries to make its simple way out of the human body. There are other desperados who lure the vulnerable traveler off-path: insecurity, anxiety, self-consciousness, the fragile ego—but nearly all are unmasked first cousins to fear when flushed out of the shadows. Some fears are linked to primal traumas, which may yet be unearthed. These deserve special attention when working with voice.

I think the greatest of all distractions between heart and throat might be faithlessness, because reigning religious institutions have effectively redirected the focus from faith to matters of righteousness, wrongness and "policies." Faith in love, and what it can do, has taken a particularly destructive backseat to the priorities of massive organizations with other things in mind than loving kindness, peaceful communication, fair resolutions, wellness, and the expressive voices of living, breathing people.

For today's spiritually traumatized, broken-hearted, and soul-wounded, the process of revealing what rests on the heart can be a paralyzing challenge. To clear the path of negative imprint, one must declare the intention to speak to what matters most and set about the task of discerning what that is. One can make a choice now to stand up to the fears that mangle the truth into expressions more palatable for others, cause explosions of rage, freezing up, or cut-and-run behavior.

To love the truth more than anything else is a tall order.

It is understandable to hide behind fear and past trauma in lieu of speaking with the intent to heal. These obstacles provide familiar comfort, acting as avoidant layovers instrumental in talking ourselves out of taking action on our behalf. Seeking effective medicine acts as a truth serum that changes us when we can name our commitment to keep relations clean and healthy, including our relationships with ourselves.

Tools that mend send a continual stream of messages to the overprotective mind saying that the spirit is in charge of what comes and goes along that highway between heart, mind, throat, and all other aspects of us. Imagine a world where our spirits governed our expressions.

A question to consider is: What are we representing, or in service to, if not the spirit's knowledge of Divine Love?

Perhaps it is fantasy to say that who we are as spiritual beings can determine what we say and to whom, but for the sake of learning something new about ourselves, let's imagine it. If we can dare to believe that we are spirits in human form, maybe it will be possible to think, say, and act with more purpose and care about the impact we're having.

On the path of uncovering tools to support the function and purpose of voice as it serves the spirit, I've also discovered that the emotions of truth need a safe place to come out to play. What yearns to be said aloud has a way of becoming more confident with practice.

I have written the prayers in the first person, in contrast to my first book, because they are personal and land more efficiently on the soul. My hope is that something will loosen and become free in you as a result of reading them this way.

It has been my experience that clearing the way with prayer guides energy up through the soles of the feet from the core of Earth and opens up the crown for divine communication to flow through. Imagine our infinite reach when we surrender ourselves to the energies of all that exists Above and Below.

The book was written in the midst of significant political, civil, and human rights upheaval here in the U.S. While writing it, an idea circled me: When requests made to the Divine are rooted in something greater than simple want, the result is that we become a source of embodied generosity to self, humanity, and the Earth (great provider of our needs that she is).

Each of the prayers is part of an intimate conversation, one that I hope will inspire you to unearth and expand upon the subject for yourself. I hope that this collection will be a strength and a comfort for you as you honor your sacred instrument: voice. I hope it will gentle your self-talk and inspire many conversations with The Source of Life As You Understand It, and with those around you.

Pixie Lighthorse
2016

FOREWORD

In every generation, there are a handful of hearts that inexorably raise the vibration for generations to come. Pixie Lighthorse has found her way into my heart and changed the way I see, feel, listen, and pray. Thanks to my parents, I always knew there was a divine force watching out for me; Pixie brings to life potent prayers to affirm that presence.

She reminds us to seek the daily learnings of love in our lives. She invites us to stand tall and listen for our highest creations, to hear others, to locate and choose what heals. She welcomes us to engage and enhance the neurological architecture of adhering to our highest form of intelligence—gratitude.

She asks us to sit more closely to what hurts, reminds us of where to rest our sometimes confused gaze, holds our hands in hers, and helps us locate the underlying meaning. She puts words to the most sublime leanings in our hearts. She gives shape to our thankfulness and then moves us to breathe into that shape and inhabit the space beyond it. She reorganizes our pain and amplifies our evolution with embodied awareness.

There is nothing more precious than a relationship with your own consciousness. When you forget, this book will help you remember to create space for devotion, empower your gratitude, and elevate your terms of engagement with all-that-is.

Thank you, Pixie, for reminding me that I've always been praying. Thank you for putting the perfect words to our holy hearts.

Elena Brower
New York

HOW TO USE THIS BOOK

VOICE is a companion to hold close to your chest as you quest to recover your sacred expressions from their hiding places. It is your humble assistant, working to create favorable conditions as you activate and advocate for causes that require championing including you. Your health and serenity are a worthy cause, as well as the health of the Earth and your loved ones. I have written it to be your partner, helpmate, and friend.

You have been communicating all your life. Experiences—especially those formed by repetitive patterns and early trauma—have a way of asking us to adjust, make concessions, put our real feelings on the back burner, bite our tongues, bind down what is vulnerable, and compromise our faith. Truths locked tightly behind closed doors rely on dynamite and heavy artillery in order to be heard. Sadly, they seem to sequester themselves away again in shame after the explosion or implosion. Our original nature has been shut down many times and our human bodies pay the price. Use this book to build your voice and return to who you were in original form.

To get the most from it, note which prayers enthuse and bring you energy. Dog-ear the ones that seem confronting and revisit them. Notice when a truth knocks persistently for your attention.

Maybe you will underline the phrases that touch your knowing. Maybe you will cross out the bits that do not present potential and growth for you. Maybe you will find that the words help you find your exact relationship to what matters to you most. Maybe you will take it to your council, your circle of loved ones, and share from it. Maybe you will tear out the pages and leave them for others to find or make art on them.

I want to welcome you to interact in any way you need to. It will help you discern what conjures an earthquake of passion within you. Maybe it will help you ask the needed questions, as well as examine the flawed political, religious, and family systems we live with.

Each section of prayers is aligned with the teachings of the Four Directions, because there are seasons in which a voice evolves: the early stages of lumps in the throat, watering eyes, and borrowed courage; the secondary stages of making a reasonable plan and taking action; the raw and humble stage of vulnerability; and the time when we are able to take a higher level of responsibility for what we communicate. If you recognize where the compass is pointing you, turn straight to that section, and work those seven prayers. Feel them out and try them on.

On the left-side blank pages, consider sketching a representation of what the prayer brings up for you, or collage the words you are envisioning yourself speaking. Write the poetry or prose that flows most easily from you. Write your angers, frustrations, and disappointments—allow the book to hold them for you. Write your own revelations.

The journal prompts at the end of each section are designed to take the reader deeper into each of the stages. Record your answers as the feelings and thoughts arise. Work with this book as you would a midwife or coach who is helping you fall in love with dialoguing with the Divine.

EAST

Season: *Spring*
Element: *Air*

In the East, the adventurer steps out onto the precipice of the unknown with unprecedented enthusiasm: the excitement of possibility, fear, trepidation, fantasies, and imaginings of what might come. It is a time to acknowledge risks, assess favorable climates, and step out of comfort zones to honor what is true. Facing the sunrise, greet the day with courage and belief in yourself. Look to others who have walked the path you want to walk and make notes. Create the roads that have yet to be paved. Point your compass in the direction of the changes you want to experience and prepare for exploration.

Honoring Risk

Thank you for this perfect day for taking chances.

Bless the heart that steps into the light tunnel of alternative thinking.

Help me understand that keeping quiet keeps me small. Guide me to compose my ideas and thoughts without worry about who will respond and how. Help me open to rejection that may come from expressing my ideas and feelings. Show me the real hazards–keep me from making up artificial ones that stall forward movement. Help me gather thoughts that come from my heart.

Support me as I face the unknown. Strengthen my relationship to uncertainty by making my foundation a pyramid. Remind me like those who've gone before me, I'm stepping out of the comfort zone to engage possibility. Redirect my fears and place my feet on the path in front of me. Give me a nudge. Help me be a bold example to others who look to me to lead with faith.

Spread my arms wide, open my heart wider, and let me find out for myself. Help me speak from love. Help the healing medicine rise in me.

Remind me that there are no healing reasons to protect those who have done harm. Help me to say the things no one can say for me. Let me remember that my admissions of what is true are as important to my own ears as they are to anyone who listens.

I am ready to pioneer a new way for myself. Pave my road with clarity and trust. Mark the trail with feathers for help soaring.

May my efforts fortify my habit of speaking up for myself. May my vow to try as many times as necessary reveal the promise of my freedom. May my mistakes be my teachers. Help me to reframe what I wish to have said more clearly and truthfully. Let me grant myself second and third opportunities.

Encourage me to stick my neck out—not onto the chopping block, but to stretch myself to beautiful lengths in order to greet what's ahead.

Honoring Humility

Thank you for this day of forgiving myself and others.

Provide me with the wisdom to strengthen my ego. Open me to feedback about how my words and actions have landed. Help me self-correct. Let me admit my wrongs and make things right. Help me make the necessary amends while finding my natural gift for compassion and mercy. Let me be teachable. Help me care about the impact I have.

Position me to honor the voices of others and let my two cents take a backseat now and again. Remind me that my loved ones are on their own journeys, and that sometimes my words of advice aren't needed. Help me know when to serve others with what I've learned and when to let them find their own ways. Let me remember that listening is a gift I give to myself, and to give it freely. Help me put down my distractions as a show of support. Help me wait for my turn.

Inspire me with your tiny ants, gray wrens, the unmajestic pea-hen—those who command attention modestly. Remind me of the powerful messages from those with quiet plumage. Show me elegance where there is no grandiose display. Remind me that there are times to make my presence known and times to pass the talking stick.

Teach me to be simple in the presence of divine opportunity in unexpected forms: a child who asks a million questions, a friend working through a dilemma the hard way, a new parent struggling with unforeseen limitations, or a social issue in need of mobilization. Gift me the ability to listen for the call to action, to accept, be grateful, warm, and welcoming of new intelligence. Instill in me the usefulness of not always knowing the answers.

Help me be an unpretentious learner. Give me the willingness to be vulnerable in my seeking state. Offer me the courage to approach those who might have a map to direct me.

Let me never possess all I need to know. Bless my quest as I listen, learn, and grow my faith in life's processes.

Honoring Love

Thank you for this day and vastly expanding the capacity of my heart. Thank you for helping me lean into the comfort of infinite love and for my ability to inspire it everywhere I go.

There are times when I cannot speak of what I love because I fear my expressions will not be appreciated, my affections not reciprocated. During these moments, help me realize that love moves in one direction—out of me—and that is all that matters. I understand that what I give out comes back in its way and not always in the form I expect. Help me trust that there is enough love for me. In the empty spaces where love has left me, let me conjure faith to be open to all forms of love, which are moving around and through me at all times.

Dress my language in the sacred robes of adoration. Fill my mouth with genuine tribute, so I can shower others generously. I know I can be an open vessel despite the ways I've been hurt. Help me remember that it is not love that has hurt me. It is the absence of love that causes the ache. Teach me to increase my commitment to love.

Help me sing the incantations of devotion and rapture as they have always existed inside of me from before my journey in this form. Help me understand that divine love is required nourishment for life to animate and flourish. Do not find me reaching to prove otherwise but keep me in service to love from this moment on.

Ease my tongue in the discourse of tenderness, further indebting myself to its worthy cause. When I am tested to fear, to hate, despise, defend, or object, press pause on my desire to rant. Remind me of humankind's greatest gift of love and that to give it when it is a challenge is to let it rule my purpose. Help me mind the mantras of high regard when I forget.

Let me learn to give and receive your most sacred treasure.

Allow me to be dogmatic about just one thing: my vow to love and the lavish, excessive distribution of it.

Honoring Spontaneity

Thank you for this day of freedom to walk an unexpected and spirited path.

I am eager to see where we can go together. Let's get lost tempting fate with frolic and impetuousness. What expressions might emerge when I am uncensored, enraptured, unpredictable, "it" in your game of tag? What will happen if my wildness is construed offensive? Come close and whisper that there is room for rebellion. Entrust me to clean up my mistakes or misspeaks, which have resulted from sudden bursts of roguishness.

Remind me, when I hesitate to follow my excitement, that magic reveals itself in unstructured movement and communication. To hold back is to forbid the dawning to occur. Tolerate my meanderings. Grant me my verbosities and explorations. Help me permit myself to know the joy in chasing amazement without over-cautiousness.

Direct me to make meaning of what lands in front of me at the crossroads. Help me speak up on behalf of others who do not have a voice. Devote me to seeking out the experiences that give birth to change and transformation and teach me to love the quest through witnessing the transformative process in myself and others.

Intrigue me. When I become too settled, shake me up. Be the delightful sounds my throat is yearning to try. Let my body dance unbridled in the way it most wants to move. Let my hands sculpt the shapes that stir up awe. I am determined to find my groove with you and grow my trust in how I show it.

Make me gritty and magical in the ways I honor life. Help me articulate my outlandish ideas and be open to varying schools of thought about how to make them real. Prepare me to be unafraid of contrast and pony me up with the skills of improvisation.

Be the spurs (of the moment) in my sides, and let's ride.

Honoring Curiosity

Thank you for this day to question everything.

Inspire me to quench my thirst for knowledge and answers. Remove my apologies for needing to ask who, what, why, and how. Expose me to the teachers who engage my mind and explain to me how it's done, how it works, how it's made, and how it's all connected. Sign me up for the course of life with the sole purpose of marveling at the wonders of the world. Strengthen me as a student of the extraordinary. Help me look behind the curtain and glimpse new worlds invisible to the bored, ambivalent, and indifferent. Activate my imagination so I may recognize and rescue treasure when I find it.

Open my mind and develop my fascination with inquiry. Heal my cluelessness. Help me observe my people and look more deeply into them. Show me their iridescent colors, their beauty; let me be willing to dig deeply with self-forged tools in order to know them in a sacred way. Let me know the Earth this way, too, and the feral creatures—the captivating biology of movement uninvolved with the pace of modern technology.

Remind me to continue my quest for natural intelligence like Raven does, studying intricacies, managing complexity, and maintaining communications with others in the kingdom. Let me turn the cranks to see what happens and examine the results with consideration.

Instill in me a determination for engagement in life—to be part of it, mixed up in it, and not a complaining spectator. Curb my cynicism and the need to have it all figured out. Disconcern me with what others think. Encourage me to investigate what I am called to know more about. Help me use my voice to formulate the questions that will crack codes and bring about even more questions.

Support my inklings and help me follow my intuition to new frontiers. Aid me in experiencing the joy that comes from removing passivity. Strengthen my muscles for scouting and rooting. Let me test my theories with you at my side.

Catch me when I fall and set me upright again.

Honoring Clarity

Thank you for this day of helping me boil it down to the essence.

Download in me the mantras that eliminate confusion. Remind me of what I'm really after on this search, which leads me around in circles and cycles. Give me the patience to hear the simplest tune of your message. Help me honor the part of me that is ready and willing to know it. Help me share the kernels that come through with a friend or two who can appreciate a good pondering. May we shed a bit of light on one another's unraveling threads.

Nurture my higher mind to override the broken model of thinking, which leads to inner and outer war. As I reach for what clarifies, help me to be open to the shifts that good medicine brings. Expand me and contract me. Guide wings around my soul to carry me up to higher reason and back. Dust off my feathers and find me weightless with remembrance of why I am here—why we are all here.

Connect my dawnings like the great constellations of the cosmos. Distill my pantheon of thoughts, hopes, and dreams into clear and flowing language ready for communication.

Inspire me to take smaller bites, digest the pieces one at a time, in a way that makes sense to me. Help me release what is not crucial to my higher relations. Whisper clues about where you want me to go, and I'll chart my way into alignment with you.

Uncloud my foggy eyes; reveal new awareness so I may be energized by the lucid direction forward. Wipe away years of accumulated programming so I may speak in my own dialect, develop my own lexicon, and distinguish who I am among others. Let me trust that the gems that sparkle brightest will help me concisely make my point.

Teach me to access the tracker in me, that which remains of my indigenous instinct. Help me follow the markers you have left for me to the answers I am seeking. Lead me back to my original spirit on a trail of peaceful knowing.

Honoring Confidence

Thank you for this day of completely believing in myself.

When I feel unsafe and insecure, I am living in chaos and out of love. When I'm confident, I am who you've made me to be. Help me see support all around me. Help me heal my existence injuries, lodged in little capsules of trauma throughout me. Help me dissolve them with the breath you've given me.

Let me call up the deepest and most electric seed of me, so I may shine with no puffing or posturing, no faking it 'til I make it, no exaggerating or inflating the truth of my accomplishments and abilities.

I am enough. I might need many reminders from you, Divine Source of Connection, to know and accept this. Thank you for pointing me to the beauty and strength inside of me.

Remind me that I can do what I set out to with everything I have in this moment. When my gifts are needed, raise my hand into the air. Fill me with faith that I will find my way, and have plenty of help. Remind me to seek education when it's truly required, but do not allow me to trick myself into believing I'm not there yet. When adventuresome service calls, let me pick up.

Help me put my gifts into words so I can represent them fairly and fully. When I'm unsure, strengthen my spine. Send awareness of my specialties rippling through each vertebra.

Help me prepare for challenges in advance. Help me to be unapologetic about what is co-created with you from love.

Remind me that insecurity is simply a belief that I am unprotected. Let my love of what we do together lift me up. When I think I'm unable—that I'm not made for this, they'd be better off without me, I don't fit here, I'm unwanted, I'm unnecessary—set me straight. We both know that these thoughts are not of you or me, but rather a powerful force that seeks to hold me back.

Help me create a world where people are safe, secure, and can enjoy a sense of belonging.

JOURNAL PROMPTS FOR THE EAST

What do I come up against when I consider taking a risk with my voice?

What past events dissuade me from proceeding?

What helps me follow my curiosity?

What would I most like to say if there would be no repercussions?

Who will support me as I try my voice out in new ways?

What do I have to gain by keeping quiet?

What might I lose if I speak what is true?

How have I protected others, sacrificed myself, or been sacrificed?

What are the benefits of advocating for myself and others?

What thoughts infuse me with confidence to step off the path others have made for me and create my own?

What am I willing to say for love?

What needs to happen before I can speak what lives inside of me?

What am I afraid will happen?

Where is trauma trapped inside of my body? Can I find new ways to release it and clear the way for improved communication throughout my systems?

SOUTH

Season: *Summer*
Element: *Fire*

In the South, the traveler is presented with options for taking action and making agreements. It is the stage in which commitment to something greater than oneself is discovered, vows are bonded, integrity determined, leaps taken, and pointed questions asked. Vision becomes reality at this stage, enabling an individual to put their talk to the test in order to walk the walk. Impeccable choices support creative journeys and prevent unnecessary detours.

Honoring Respect

Thank you for this day of reverent growth.

I am seeking new ways to respect myself, you, the Earth, and my dear ones. I'm asking for help to know what I value and treat it right. I'm asking for solid support in building my vocabulary and increasing my range to address all that I cherish. As I take inventory of those I deeply admire, teach me to see myself as worthy of high regard. Drive me to notice where I can develop keen listening and speak to my people with great care and consideration.

Help me speak with sacredness on my mind. When I don't agree with what is being said, turn up my ability for high-frequency communication and awareness to the level I would most love to receive when I am in the same position. Coat my larynx in the language of conserving and protecting what is truly precious. Do not discover me traveling well-worn paths of resentment. Cultivate in me a terminology of sticking to the point and help me see verbal violations as utterly dysfunctional.

Help me receive the sentiment behind the words, because few will be able to say it like I want to hear it. For those I adore, build tolerance in me to tap into the sweetness they attempt to convey. Protect them from my haphazard accusations of crimes they didn't commit. Help me remember why I love them and why we are in relationship. Reform our bonds and raise my level of integrity. Remind me to offer confidentiality when called for and hold the intimacies of my beloveds with trust.

I love this world and all-natural things in it. Let me see myself and those close to me as part of that immense organic beauty. Lead me in the ways of preserving and protecting what I value. Concern me less with the stories holding me accountable. Let respect inform my actions. Help me acknowledge where I can pay more tribute. Warm my heart with a flame of reverence and gratitude for all living things. Establish in me the depth of recognition for all that needs my support.

I am able and willing to give it. Sock it to me.

Honoring Honesty

Thank you for this day of making it safer than ever to tell the truth.

Help me honor myself and others by taking the time to get clear about my part in what happened, what's at work, where it went wrong, and what can make it right. Help me communicate cleanly, without projection and blame. I need your assistance to cut through my illusions and facades: to value the truth above all else–and give it a rightful place in my throat. Be the sword that carves away the false fear of what I must protect.

Help me value outspokenness over convenience and my impulsive desire for a different reality. Give me courage when I avoid confronting myself about a matter that requires attention. Help me declare my needs without negating others'.

Hold me up when I'm disappointed in myself and don't want to hurt anyone with the truth of my actions. Curtail my drive to manipulate the facts in order to make myself appear stronger, better, or more clever. Help me know my part and take responsibility for the conditions I may have created that led to disharmony. Diffuse my shame. Dose me with right medicine so I am directed by my willingness to resolve the matter. Show me the price of betraying myself or others with false accounting.

Position me for balance by helping me make bold declarations about who I am, what I want, who I can help, and how to be of service.

Guide me to create safe relationships where I can be forthcoming about my own nature and welcoming to those stepping forward, too. Help me release my judgment when a loved one comes clean. Teach me how to create secure spaces throughout my life where truth is free to breathe and thrive. Teach me not to recoil from information that hurts, but to be brave for withstanding the storms of actuality.

Help me develop trust by being honest with myself, removing obstacles and forming a broad, stable base at the root of me where it has been eroded over time.

Honoring Advocacy

Thank you for this day of progressive perception.

Help me speak out for justice with a special desire fueled by a power greater than surface comforts and outdated systems.

Let me be a troublemaker to champion those I love and care for, and for those I don't know intimately who need my help. Hire me to be a powerful voice for the change that heals, reconciles, forgives, and improves. Help me create time and space to lend support where it is needed. Rigorously stir my passion to be deeply bothered by violations to life, liberation, happiness, and voice. Find me faithful and in service, riding shotgun to heart-led movements, and leading the charge when it's up to me to do so. Remove my feelings of hopelessness in who I perceive to be the opposition. Align me with action and channel my energy for others.

Bind me to the medicine of love. Let me affect the transformation that leads to needed change. Light the torch of revolution in my heart. Stand me upright on a foundation of faith while I take the next steps. Build my voice as an instrument for defending freedoms, which provide equality. Keep my motivations clean. Grant me the tools to see near and far and adjust my lens OFTEN.

Help me give a leg up to the underdog and root for the one who doesn't stand a chance. Help me accept being unliked or misunderstood for positioning myself behind who and what I believe in.

Bolster my confidence and give me the understanding and empathy required for sustainable action. Make tolerance my priority and give me the words to fight violence with the sword of peace.

Orient me to inclusivity. Help me stop putting individuals into dualistic opposition, rather focus me on repairing mistakes, and my participation in them. Dissolve my tendencies for cliques, partisanship, judgment, righteousness, bandwagons, and the damning or idolizing of those I perceive to have more than me.

Help me do my part to clang the bells of freedom.

When ten thousand are whispering, make me one who is listening.

Honoring Practice

Thank you for this day of ritual devotion.

Guide me to the mat, the trail, the teapot, the canvas, and the confrontation table today, so I may test my flexibility and stay true to my form all the way to my edge. Be my mirror, my educator in matters of discipline and rhythm. Open the shelter of my mind to constructive, caring feedback.

Let all that comes to me be my teachers. Move my form and feelings with dedicated habit. Help me rehearse for growing stronger and more resilient. Stand me up like a mountain: spread my arms wide, expanding and clearing the valves of my heart to help me move from it. Point my fingers skyward and widen my stance. Wrap enormous wings around my legs to strengthen my rooted position.

Train me for the battle, which takes place within me in the form of fear and resistance. Help me create spaciousness inside of my container to make steady progress with my breath, my invocations, and the attitudes that initiate my day. Lead air into my lungs, which comforts the grief held there. Enhance my supportive routines with the golden light of your encouragement that shines through repetition. Let my body be a living ceremony.

When I wander, bring me back to presence. Help me refocus without shame when I lose my way. Make me brave to notice where my balance falters, and I compromise my integrity. Rededicate me when I discover what I'm holding and protecting. Get me back on conscious feet when I fall. Let my wingspan be the bridge between my spirit and my body. Ignite the fire of my willingness during times of challenge and overcoming obstacles.

Put in front of me those who will help me persevere in my attempts to effectively resolve inner and outer conflict. Remind me of my tools for perceiving what prevents my flow. Help me be attentive to my part in maintaining the quality of relationship I am called to cultivate. Help me puzzle together my healing form with the help of Earth's electricity moving upward through the soles of my feet.

Let me know I am not alone and that I never need to do it perfectly.

Honoring Creation

Thank you for this day of making and forging.

Hone my craft. Lead my hands and thoughts to paper, canvas, clay, instruments, and gardens. Let sacred expression funnel through me to the working surface. Help me convey the messages I am wishing to unearth. Light the lamp at the seat of my soul, so I might further investigate my range of commentary and vision. Let the creative fire in me open the portals of my imagination. Help me create the forms, shapes, and lines that spark a rendezvous between you and me.

Disconcern me with the sacred works of others so what comes forth from me is unique. Let me mind my business with you, adorning the canvas with my marks as demonstrated in every tree, stone, and cloud. Expand my ability to arrange the elements in a way that represents my vibration. Answer my questions of who I am as a creative being—who I was designed to be. Help me find the ways to raise the energy that sustains me.

Through my inventive problem-solving, reveal the originality in my works. Show me my gifts, talents, and skills. Let me love what I do with them. Emphasize how to do this, as I don't always know where to begin except to keep my hands moving. Put me with like-mindeds who also want to receive and interact with divine inspiration.

Unclog my blocks and release the barriers that hold back my flow of light and color, darkness and sensation. Turn off the radio of both compliments and critiques. Let me focus on what you have me doing. Warm me with the patience to see my creations all the way through—be they children, musical compositions, seedling starts, pots, or paintings. Shush my thoughts of giving up when frustrated. Encourage me to stay with what comes naturally through me. Make me a generator, not just of beautiful things for fancy's sake, but also things that affect, move, help, solve, and confront.

Let me be content with what I can create from my faithful heart and the simplest of tools.

Honoring Vows

Thank you for this day of preserving promises.

Many treaties have been broken with myself, my partners, the earth, and you. Let me forge new bonds, so I may follow through and do what I say I'm going to. From this point forward, let me honor those I am bonded to. Help me remember what it feels like to experience fractured trust and not destroy trust between myself and others out of misunderstanding and projection. Instead, guide me to see agreements I've made as efforts to build something greater for us than the simple sum of parts, though I might fumble in the early stages. Recommit me when I do.

Join me with compatible associates I can work in concert with to bind the good medicine of what will be formed. Sanction the contracts I say YES to with firm handfastings of commitment to the union I am growing. Help me collaborate with my spirit. I will need the patience only you can give me to speak up about unfairnesses and concessions. Prevent resentment from building in me and provide me with the relational skills I need to communicate needed adjustments. Send capable mediators to establish understanding. Help me release my grudges and take responsibility for fulfilling my end of the bargain. Teach me the art of compromise and mutuality.

Help me see that when I make an agreement, the entity grows a soul of its own. Be very clear with me when it is time to unmake the mergers. When I am at a crossroads, lead me to the next path that marks a new way for me. Let me leave no loose ends or strings behind. Cut the cords with grace when my pacts are complete. Remind me that I can ask the same of those organizations that break ties with me or my people. Reconcile my sympathies in order to make clean detachments. Remind me that part of honoring my contracts also means honoring when they are fulfilled.

Connect me with a yoke of integrity when I get into bed with someone. Liberate me when liabilities are settled. Heal my heart of injury when the space of loss is felt. Strengthen my dedication to see through what I begin.

Honoring Song

Thank you for this day of precious song-keeping.

Fill my lungs with willingness. Elevate my boldness for making the historic sounds of exaltation. Let me sing out from all that is holy within me. Marry me in a ceremonial chorus with all living things. Remind me that a little tune can be a gift that touches souls and moves mountainous emotions. Be there when I forget that each creature on Earth has its own singing voice. Help me find my melody.

Help me go easy on myself when I am off-key. I may have to offend the spirits a bit while I am learning a new way to behold the seasons, my people, the land, the creatures, and the ancestors. Let it sound flat and imperfect. Let it sound wretched and jarring— if that's what it takes. My voice will soften as I repeat the ritual. Let me sing for years before expecting that my voice and tone will sound magnificent. Turn my ears away from dark messengers who maintain that I sound like an injured animal. Let this be the moment I begin to write and sing the songs that honor the beauty of life.

Magnify my range. Exhaust my pipes. Let me chant my heart's wishes for the world and harmonize with others who are courageous enough to make music with their voices. Lift us up to unify and alter the energy of the planet. Help me create the compositions that deeply heal what spoken words cannot touch.

Teach me, as you would a child, to lift up my voice without fear or apprehension. Teach me to sing gratitudes for what I have and serenade the plant and animal nations who nourish the people. Teach me to raise a generation of children to hum the sacred songs of love and remembrance.

Show me what happens to a creature when it is sung to. Help me know how sound travels and how it changes us as it lands. Show me the tears of someone who has never heard their name crooned to the heavens, so I will know the impact of what a voice can do.

Be my courage to belt the anthems beating the drum of my heart.

JOURNAL PROMPTS FOR THE SOUTH

What was said to me that still hurts?

Where have I sacrificed self-respect so as not to rock the boat for another?

Where can I find resources that will serve my purpose?

In what healthy venues can I practice speaking my values and mission?

How can I expand my range of communication?

Who would I like to hear me?

What must I shift, change, or grow for myself in order to be heard?

What must I do in order to stand strong in the face of conflict and confrontation?

How must I care for myself during the rehabilitation of my voice?

How can I rebuild trust where there is brokenness or betrayal?

What song is in my heart to sing?

WEST

Season: *Autumn*
Element: *Water*

In the West lies a host of personal, social, and cultural challenges: shadows, difficulty, doubt, weariness, grief, and the need for restoration. It is also the stage at which emotions are explored and excavated to determine the origin of motivations. When learning to effectively examine beliefs holding the quester hostage, opportunities begin to open up. This crossroads presents the chance to clean the path of psychic debris and gain clarity at the emotional level. Wading through the murkier aspects of self-sabotage offers strength and support, allowing for the release of long-held patterns.

Honoring Worth

Thank you for this day of knowing my value.

It is not for others to reflect my merits back at me. You've tried to transmit this to me many times, but it's hard to hear and easily forgotten. Help me remember that it's a miracle to be here. Drum into my cells that I don't have to carry anxiety about my value.

Expand my limits for accepting my majestic existence. Let me hang medals of honor on my own jacket and stop questioning whether I do enough and give enough. Open me to my flaws and imperfections, because my obsession with perfection is killing my spirit and faith in Divine Love. When hunger for external affirmation is insatiable, it complicates and compromises my relationships. Help me let my people off the hook for needing ideal words that will lead to my fulfillment. Freedom from inaccurate beliefs about myself is between you and me.

Help me discover how I can be most useful, knowing that my spiritual significance isn't rooted in what I do. Remove thoughts that I'm burdensome or a hindrance to those around me, or my gifts are unappreciated. Help me create a meaningful, dignified life and establish trust with you that I'm right on path. When I'm dependent on others, let me be self-sufficient. Help me define how I show up and what I can contribute. Remind me that lives are not measured in dollars.

When I'm not honoring my missions, direct me back to them. Point my generosity and kindness facing outward, knowing that everything that flows from me creates a ripple. Remind me that it's possible to trigger unworthiness in others when I set unfair and impossible standards for myself. Let "adequate" and "good enough" challenge my efforts for excellence. Highlight my benevolence, because big-heartedness is what I want to be remembered for above all.

Help me know and trust that I am a beneficial organism in the great cosmic design.

Honoring Sorrow

Thank you for this day of open suffering.

I am so sad about some things that have happened. It is unnerving that I cannot unmake them. Show me a place where I am free to express my mourning for as long as it takes. Put me in circles of others enduring ceaseless pain and help us to shelter one another in care and flowing witness. Bless me with permission to feel the scars of the swords that have flayed me open. Grant mercy for my heartache as I travel this mysterious blue landscape. Help me navigate with purpose.

I do not need to make meaning of it. There may not be an understanding I can ever come to that will transmute the agony, but if there is, I know you will show me the way. Let me lie quietly in your lap, among the bones of the ancestors powdered to dust beneath me. I need them to hold me and impart their wisdom about how to take the next step when I am ready. Let me forgive myself for my faults and the neglects that brought about the break with my spirit, my beloved, my child, or my childhood.

Help me articulate the nature of my grievances and offer them up to the heavens, not to hurry up and get over them, but to ask for small spaces of respite between the waves. Ease the stress and anxiety of my unanswerable whys about my unbearable losses. Carry them for just a little while, so I may feel the weight lighten with the understanding that I don't have to heave the burdens of my heart alone. Give my hands a rest from wringing.

Soften my face, so I may see that I am still here underneath these big feelings. Unravel my worries about whether it might always be this way. Keep me present to my healing process. Help me engage my grief with consciousness. Remind me that every tear shed comes from the tribunal source of life, the river of my vulnerable heart.

Teach me to be the one to release the torment of generations behind me and the one who wails for all of our losses.

Open my spirit for the great exchange between you and me over this.

Honoring Rage

Thank you for this day to get it up and out.

I am mad as hell. Help me scream, shout, and vindicate. Can you hold it for me? Can you hear every righteous, venomous, unreconciled indignance? Will you accept the details of my anger? Let me empty out my container of fury on your altar. It may be that the injustice that caused such a storm just needs to be heard and understood. Bear witness to my boiling blood.

I might spit and seethe until scarlet. I may curse the day I was born, or he was born, or she was born, or the day I died, or he died, or she died. Shake my red-hot fist at the one(s) who let the wrong thing happen, who didn't protect me, who didn't care, and who didn't do all they could to stop it. Strike me lightning-fast with the words to describe exactly what it feels like now. Release from me the monster into which my rage has grown, and let it feed on me no more.

Spare my loved ones what has unknowingly become toxic inside of me. Take my wrath and do what you will with it, so I can keep my relationships clean. I want to honor my life as it is today, not resent it for what it was yesterday. Show me how to surrender every bit of it to you. I do not want my dearest people to pay for what was done to me.

Help me when I begin to spin. Help me see that the trapped pain inside of me is still fighting for control. While letting my spirit lead, I want to honor the reasons for my rage.

Be there when my eyes clear, the thunderclouds part, and the layers shed—as I give voice to what I've been holding in for too long. Let me hold the black mass in my gentle hands and weep over it, giving thanks that I have overcome the ordeal of carrying it. Press the weight of it into my palms, so I may feel how heavy it has made me. Hear me growl and roar as I heave my encumbrance to the Earth.

Remind me how to lay my rage at the roots as an offering, trusting that new life will grow.

Honoring Anxiety

Thank you for this remarkable day of breathing through it.

Thank you for the tension, that I may learn from it by noticing how my body reacts and responds. Help me make the courageous choice to move my body in ways that alleviate the physical struggle of losing my breath. Take the fight and flight out of me with your comforting, nurturing voice. Help me know the difference between my perception of threat and the actual thing. Remove me gently from situations, schedules, and scenarios that cause tightness in my chest and lumps in my throat. Help me regroup and return to try again.

Ease my discomfort with tools that work. Elevate my feet for blood flow, which supports circulation through my heart. Prompt me to step away from triggersome moments so I can attend them with confidence. Help me to be responsible for the debilitating whirl that causes me to lose focus. Help me to diffuse the energy of worry that lodges in my system. Move my feet toward nature, where I can find my holy ground again. Place me in the current, which carries me softly forward and reminds me not to wear myself out swimming against it. Help me break it down, trace it back, and discover new ways to cope.

When it seems like everyone around me has it together, emphasize that I am not alone in my battle. Give me compassion for others who nervously retreat and offer them understanding.

Calm the butterflies that swarm my gut when I am apprehensive. Help me recognize when the panic is creeping in. Encourage me to trust that I can speak the simplest words about what is happening and be effective. When dread takes over, quiet my doubts, which intimidate and cripple me. Keep me in my body as I pass through the bottleneck. Put the healers on my path who can help me learn that I will be okay.

Put a balm of higher wisdom on my delicate heart when the familiar restlessness tries to steer the ship.

Honoring Fear

Thank you for this day of awareness of my intense desire to flee.

My fears are stopping me—keeping me small and hidden in a corner. Stand me up and set me free from this tiny room of shadows, where my voice wavers and my shoulders shudder. Help me call them out and name them—beckon them forward so I may face them. Be my strength when I order them to back down.

When my throat locks up and silence hangs thick on my tongue, energize me with your bright blue light of courage. Arm me with a sword of light to slice through the illusions I mistake for beliefs. Train me to dodge their advances with the mastery of spiritual aikido and deflect them with cuffs of gold. Train me for battle with my worries, troubles, imprints and memories.

Smoothly guide me through the challenges and anxieties of the unknown. Re-define my relationship to uncertainty. Light up the room with a glimpse of life on the other side of these consuming and irrational discouragements. Remind me that few of my fears actually come true, and even if they have, it doesn't mean they always will. Equip me not for the worst that can happen but with determination to take all things into consideration with a reasonable and quiet mind–no shrinking back reflexively. Give me pause to reflect before reacting. Let me listen with the heart of a loving parent to the part that's afraid to cross the shaky bridge.

Let me not be daunted by a devouring sensation of fright, but instead thank it audibly for its cautionary attempt to protect me from harm. Let me learn a new way to console my fears and talk myself through the process. Demonstrate how I can gently dismantle terror and soothe my uneasiness with the wisdom of what I know to be true.

Let my voice feel the fright and speak anyway. It's okay if it trembles. It will not always be this way if I practice.

Help me understand what it will be like to be free and take measured steps to get there. Fill me with assurance and hope.

Honoring Depth

Thank you for this day of submergence.

Willingly escort me into my ancient inner well to retrieve the good medicine. Challenge me to share about my secret places—the cavernous regions that select few are invited into. Guide me to choose my listeners with care, keeping company today with those who have examined their shadowy undercurrents and offered to be safe havens. Help me gather closely with those who do not fear the chasms and recognize them as fellow divers who know the terrain of the holy well. Help me trust that the flood will not drown me, but open me to the sacredness of life.

Let my journey into what lies beneath the surface be rewarding. Help me appreciate the weight of my wild and enduring spirit, traumas, and vulnerabilities. Engulf me in trust for my ability to hold this space inside of me—rich with memories, offerings, and passions. Enable those who know my depths to reflect my magic back at me. Commit me to reciprocity. Help me accept people as works-in-progress. Dissolve my judgment when invited into their watery dimensions. Teach me to see the best in them and myself.

Help me move beyond the programming that instructs me to share only what's on the surface. Grant me the concentration to stay with myself when I'm opening up and allow myself to be heard and known. Discourage me from peeking into the portal, then slamming it shut again out of fear or pride. Tolerate no stonewalling or sullenness. When I cling to the shallows, provide me with the resources and support to dive deeper. Kindle in me a desire to know myself thoroughly and see kindred relationships as encouragement to forego the frivolous.

Protect my energy as I venture down with others. Plunge me not into mean-spirited communication, where shadows are tools that perpetuate dysfunction. Help me engage and exchange intimacies and ideas respectfully. Help me be met with equal intensity and passion.

Strengthen me to discern fact from fallacy and depth from delusion and keep moving.

Honoring Transformation

Thank you for this beautiful day of changing.

My shell is shifting, my skin shedding, and I am uncomfortable with what is leaving me. Help me find the language to describe the discarding, the baring of my branches. Bring understanding so I can welcome what is coming. When I am unsure about how to go forward, help me prepare for my new stage. Help me trust that I will love myself through it. When the time is optimum, encourage me to let go of what has passed.

When those around me are not eager to know my restored, original spirit, soften me with the realization that if I am uncomfortable with my changing, they must be, too. Let me be an example of becoming more whole while I am leaving unneeded parts of my previous shape behind. Startle my senses with cellular renewal, awakening my purpose and direction. Move me through the dark nights and ease the pain of liquification inside the chrysalis. Excavate my soul's gestural poetry and help me find what is next with fluid movement. Unfurl my damp, untested wings and lift my willingness to the limitless skies.

Rouse my interest in the world I am seeing with newborn vision. Reinforce my sacred commerce with the Divine. Guide my hands to build altars to the portals of existence I can now pass through with ease. Protect me as I construct relationships that are more complex than those I have previously known. Strengthen my small shelter in the woods, my room of one's own to re-create, re-invent, and re-imagine.

Help me weave healing medicine with my acquired gifts and experiences. Harmonize my fresh layer with knowing the meaning of this shift. Ease me through the other side and set me down delicately to fully embody my unusual, more-me form. Clear me of any blockages that stop the flow of goodness from me and the flow of goodness to me.

Salt me with grateful tears and cleansing rain. Bathe me in the distilled waters of evolution.

JOURNAL PROMPTS FOR THE WEST

Where does resistance gather and pool inside of me?

What prevents me from moving forward?

What patterns in my family ancestry are repeating in me?

Which of my griefs need to be tended?

How have I neglected or abandoned my voice?

Where can I find reliable support for the emotions that hold me hostage and hiding?

What skills can I improve to help overcome difficulty?

What training do I need to help change my programming?

How does it feel to face my dark or negative emotions?

What is the benefit of acknowledging old wounds?

NORTH

Season: *Winter*
Element: *Earth*

In the North, the sojourner acknowledges the divine and earthly relevance of experience. The humble servant, who has gained wisdom by overcoming obstacles, has the opportunity to sit quietly on the Earth in reflection. By observing what has come to pass with a panoramic perspective, the journey's value is understood. To embody what has been learned is to enjoy the triumph of making it to the top of the mountain. To responsibly consider experiential wisdom is to honor life. To access the spiritual quality of the human existence is to celebrate what is infinite in each of us.

Honoring Sensuality

Thank you for this day of terrestrial bliss. It is truly heaven to be on Earth.

Speak to me of the beauty in sensitivity. Help me listen to what is influencing my barometer. Guide me out of my head and down into the valleys of my own body, mirror of the earth. Torch my nerves with the scents and sounds of life. Remove my self-consciousness. Release my familiar self-criticisms that thwart the delight of living in this temple of bone and flesh.

Help me determine what I love and how I love it. Give me the words to declare it. Remind me of what is repellent to my senses. Teach me to recognize and turn away from it. Remind me that I get a say. Legitimize my desires without needing to prove that I deserve them. Infuse me with bold self-possession. Send energy through the wide base of my roots up to the calm, smooth aperture of my throat.

Move my body in the ways that connect me to where I came from. Stretch my tissue and make me flexible. Extend my range beyond the familiar edge. Activate the energy that relates me to the infinite. Steady my feet in the dirt, and plant me firmly. Position my limbs like the tree that knows my name, the name you call me. Place a raven in the branches to beckon me taller, bolder, more assured.

Engage my beingness in the here and now. Call up the sounds that match the feelings, my lips the vehicle for endorsing my right medicine. Send in the vibrant tones that calibrate me to the eternal. Blow my hair with your winds and catch my breath as I hum your presence into me. Polish my skin with the salty sweat of my efforts.

Lay me down on the soft soil to smell the pleasure of creation.

Shine your moonlight into my open crown in divine approval.

Honoring Maturity

Thank you for this day of cultivating the sureness only experience can provide.

Thank you for getting me to the foot of the mountain. Help me climb it, slowly and patiently, to sit upon the mesa and overlook the seasons of growth and development I have known. Curate the words I speak and let me share my trials and adventures. Help me use discretion and filter out what will not be helpful. Remind me that there is no need to flaunt that I have been there and done that.

Build my ego strength so I can speak without shame—from the place in me that cares about what I convey, but not whether there is a satisfying response. Drape a shawl of emotional intelligence around my shoulders and bow me humbly to the earth in service.

Move my tongue with tact and grace, diplomacy and composure— not reactivity or defensiveness. Make my case strong for what matters most. Give me the vigilance to stand for something, and plant it in those who will take it forward. Help me channel the goodness I have come to know and direct it sincerely. Give me the authority to protect what is precious: time, energy, and finite resources. Help me share what has allowed me to be self-sufficient, while providing for those in my care.

Let me trust my words not because of my age, but because I have proven myself to be fair and equitable. Work me overtime to gain that trust. Bring attention to how I speak to those in my footpath and help me ease their learning curve without robbing them of their necessary journeys. Affirm my milestones by expanding my openness to sharing what I know. Grow me into ripeness through providence. Help me sprout hope in those around me by sharing what has worked, not delivering warnings about what did not. Raise my ambitions for a world that is safe to live in and help me engineer it.

Compose me with the grit you will return me to.

Honoring Responsibility

Thank you for this day of raising the bar.

Focus my attention on where I need to show up and how. Concern me with the consequences of my actions. Help me reconcile the mistakes causing suffering now. Help me address the issues and make me accountable for coming up with solutions. Contract me to listen for the call to address the overarching problems with what I have to offer. Show me how to skillfully work with the energy present to create a new way. Call in the brass.

Take my inventory. When I have wronged someone in word or deed, put me in the hot seat. Help me set things right again. Remind me how easy it is to self-correct when my priority is love.

Let me have the fortitude to face another's pain and give empathy even when I cannot relate. Help me comprehend the seriousness of another's conditions and bring my pledge to the table. Let me honor myself as a mediator and healer where I can be of help by cultivating honest and loving accountability. Make me answerable for what I have set in motion.

Help me create a foundation from which to act heroically when called to.

Amplify the quality of my connection to the people in my life. Sharpen my travel between the things I don't yet understand and what I am being shown. Show me the relationships between actions and results.

Help me make good use of what you have given me, by helping me to maintain an attitude of reverence for what is sacred. Help me see all life as infinitely dimensional, existing far beyond my scope of vision, and to negotiate the space that lies between us.

Obligate me to restore balance. Seat me at the table of humble servants and show me what needs to happen.

I'll do it.

Honoring Security

Thank you for this day of spiritual grounding.

Untie me from the ship previously lost at sea and place my feet on solid ground. Earth me in what I know to be true—all I have been taught that has served me well. Lift my eyes to recognize and take in what supports and sustains me. Surround me with the wealth of community, the abundance of nature, and the prosperity of fulfillment.

Imagine me a hunter of the soul's treasures, returning with sound intelligence for sharing at the home hearth. Help me reach my potential as your gardener and preservationist by placing me regularly among the plants and animals.

In a circular gesture of receiving and giving back through the seasonal turns, help me till into the soil that which feeds and nurtures it to health. Let me mother those who find me on trail, as I have been held and encouraged by you and those special loved ones who saw my need. Let me repay the favor. Let me value others and hold them in high regard. Let me witness the deepest promise of greatness in each living creature I meet. Let me believe in the fruit that has yet to be born from them and support them with friendship.

Show me my purpose so I may celebrate and value the work I've done while enjoying the simple pleasures of spirited exchange among my kind. Remind me of what it took to get here. Regenerate my energy. Educate me in the economics of harmony. Retrain my rhythm to the heartbeat of the ground that cradles me. Run with my spirit through the fields of revelry and let me never forget that I belong to you. Bless me with the immodest songs of merriment and gaiety. My days of hesitancy are behind me.

Surrender me to the ambition of the mountain—my final destination of this quest. Lodge within my banks of reason the fact that I am provided for in all ways. Remind me that I am of you, my sister and brother, too.

Accept our thanks for all of creation and for this journey.

Honoring Grace

Thank you for this day of forgiving myself and others.

It is in you that I find the simplicity in breaking ties with what I once held too tightly. You have whispered pardons for my mistakes. Now I will gift others and myself the same. Thank you for providing me with countless examples of acquittal to follow throughout my life. You have shown me that life is much too short for clutching.

For the words that have been said with intent to harm me, let me leave them at the gate before walking through my door. For the words I have said that have injured, let me make amends as soon as possible. For the words I never said, but needed to, let me say them now—first to you for clarity, and then to those they are meant for. For the words that were never said to me, but which needed to be, let me say them to myself, bury my expectations of others and move forward.

For the times when I have judged, let me look in the mirror. For the times when I have felt judged, release my impulse to be a victim. For the times when I have made a critical error, let me correct my course. For the times when I have efforted to no avail, let me keep trying.

In response to shame, let me unhinge the habit by not shaming in return. In response to guilt, let me acknowledge the poor choice and make it right. In response to fragmentation, help me retrieve my lost parts, integrate, and reassemble. In response to violations of my boundaries, let me put more effective ones in place and blame no one for coming through the holes in my fences.

Thank you for the ability to come from integrity as my spirit dictates, to be a house of sanctuary. Thank you for helping me know where I stand and helping others know what they can expect from me.

Honoring Observation

Thank you for this day of watchfulness.

Give me the perception to notice the changes taking place inside of me. Help me see them clearly reflected in my environment. Take me deep into the hermitage of my spirit to ponder the here and now, and foresee the coming challenges. Purify my filters so I can understand my connection to all living things and my place in this Universe.

Align my attentions with the stars and all that lies beyond this form. Illuminate me with the glow of contemplation. Let me study what I see on the ground long before I come to conclusions and longer before I speak. Bless me with an untroubled, uncrowded mind as I bring the whole picture into radical focus.

As I witness the unfoldment of the world before me, help me consider everything at work. Swell my vision by showing me the critical moving parts in this constellation of life. Soften my brow. Help me hold my gaze. Allow me to glimpse the shapeshifting of evolution.

Allow my meditations to produce the kind of stillness that spots the detection of movement. Calm my fears about what I see. Show me the light and the dark, the forward movement and the setbacks. Show me the Oneness that lies above and beyond opposing ideas. Let me tune in to all channels in order to derive refined insights and evaluations.

When I am ready to communicate, let me be sure that I will be heard by those who care to conference about such findings. Err me on the side of brevity and help me gather comrades who appreciate and can offer their clear deductions, as well.

Monitor my heartbeat, which echoes in time with Earth. Beat a drum inside me that connects the soil to the skies. Help me pay attention to the signs of nature so I may be an interpreter between She and the villages of people, asking that each give to one another in equal amounts.

Honoring Restoration

Thank you for this day of tranquil noiselessness. I'm grateful to be without sound, to close up shop and recharge my healthy, well-used voice.

Let no one mistake my muteness for reticence. Let my monologues be shared another time, trusting that the very good ideas that surface will return when I plug back in.

Commit me to the ceremony of fasting from language.

Press pause on my thoughts and concerns. Help me tune out all but the radiant resonance of my being. Connect me to my breath and ease the chatter of my mind. Give me a quiet place to lie down and indulge the sacred.

Dismiss my desire to work things out, jump up to write something down, and tend the many loose ends. Let everything drain out of me and into the Earth.

Allow me to restore and soothe my senses under a midnight moon or on the soft sand of a shoreline. Calm the space around my voice box, the hands I gesture with when speaking, and the spine that works hard to hold my body upright. Hush the room I stay in and pacify me into neutrality. Melt me down and seal me inside a womb of peace.

Alleviate all interference with only my deep sigh of appreciation for these downy accommodations to reconstitute my spirit. Let me enjoy the luxury of this babble-free cavern to find my still point. Allow me to rest in dis-involvement, apart from competing talk and hungry ears. Let my dreams wander inside the healing shelters of my ancestors. May the elders wave their smoking herbs over me and retrieve long-forgotten knowledge.

When I emerge, give me time to communicate my fresh understanding through the soul of my new eyes. Remind me that sound isn't the only way to share the news.

Help those close to me be comforted by my renewed presence and help me make it possible for them to retreat for needed reset, too.

JOURNAL PROMPTS FOR THE NORTH

Where do I feel most at ease with myself?

What can I do to merge my body with my spiritual experience?

What has awakened in me?

What makes me truly happy?

What passions have I discovered that I wasn't aware of before now?

How can I be of service to those who are in need?

What have I learned and developed that I can now offer to others?

What more do I need in order to feel held by something greater than myself?

Where is my magic found?

What are my most effective tools for clear communication?

How can I boldly share what I care about most with the world?

ACKNOWLEDGMENTS

I am grateful for the endless support for *Prayers of Honoring* from those who are working to heal prayer trauma and develop their conversational ways with Divine Source. I am deeply grateful to be able to put these words out into the world, and to those who find ways to utilize the prayers in unconventional and sometimes surprising applications. Thank you for your creativity.

With profound gratitude to Elena Brower, Annie Adamson and the Yoga Union Community, Melody Ross, Twozdai Hulse, Stacy de la Rosa, Betsy Cordes, Pauline, Cinnamon, Katie, Tiffanie, Mijanou Montealgre, Alexandra Franzen, and the brave women of SouLodge Sacred Voice with Raven E-Course.

Thank you, Dad, for helping me say it brave and straight.

Immeasurable thanks to Sky Sharp for your enduring commitment and belief in this project. All of my projects.

Forever and ever appreciations to Miles and Ivy for your patience and love. Thank you for caring deeply about people and Earth, enough to keep me rich in hope for the rest of life.

Cherie Dawn Carr is the author of five books centered on self-healing through intimate relationship with the natural world. She is an enrolled member of the Choctaw Nation of Oklahoma. She writes as Lighthorse to honor the unheard voices of her ancestors.

Other Books by Pixie Lighthorse

Prayers of Honoring

Prayers of Honoring Grief

Boundaries & Protection

Goldmining the Shadows

Made in the USA
Monee, IL
03 February 2023

27040257R10073